the source

arrangements for worship groups

book 5

C instruments

arranged by Chris Mitchell

Kevin Mayhew

We hope you enjoy the music in this book.
Further copies of this and the other books in the series are available
from your local music shop or Christian bookshop.

In case of difficulty, please contact the publisher direct:

The Sales Department
KEVIN MAYHEW LTD
Rattlesden
Bury St Edmunds
Suffolk IP30 0SZ

Phone 01449 737978
Fax 01449 737834
E-mail info@kevinmayhewltd.com

Please ask for our complete catalogue of outstanding Church Music.

First published in Great Britain in 1998 by Kevin Mayhew Ltd.

© Copyright 1998 Kevin Mayhew Ltd.

ISBN 1 84003 126 3
ISMN M 57004 209 8
Catalogue No: 1470305
0 1 2 3 4 5 6 7 8 9

Cover designed by Jaquetta Sergeant

Music arrangements by Chris Mitchell

Music setting by Chris Mitchell and Lynwen Davies

Printed and bound in Great Britain by
Caligraving Limited Thetford Norfolk

Contents

This index gives the first line of each hymn. If a hymn is known by an alternative title, this is also given, but indented and in italics.

CHRIS MITCHELL is a well-established arranger, composer, musical director and session musician who has worked with Graham Kendrick, David Peacock, Gloria Gaynor and the BBC. He and his wife, Linda, are experienced worship leaders and are involved in providing seminars and workshops for Christians in the arts.

401 O Lord, you're beautiful

Keith Green

2 verses

Flowing

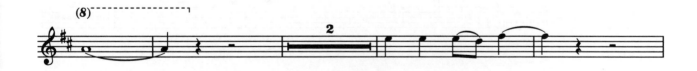

402 O Lord, your tenderness

Graham Kendrick

403 On a hill far away
(The old rugged cross)

George Bennard

4 verses

404 Once in royal David's city

Henry John Gauntlet

6 verses

405 One heart, one voice, one mind

David Hadden

406 One shall tell another
(The wine of the kingdom)

Graham Kendrick

3 verses

Lightly, with increasing pace

407 One thing I ask

Andy Park

Prayerfully

408 Only by grace

Gerrit Gustafson

Gently

Only by grace can we... enter... By

to continue | last time
Fine

1. | 2. *D.C. al Fine*

409 On this day

Wes Sutton

3 verses

410 On this day of happiness
(Three part harmony)

Graham Kendrick

411 Open the doors of praise

Ian White

With energy

412 O the blood of Jesus

Unknown

This arrangement © Copyright 1998 Kevin Mayhew Ltd.

413 O the blood of my Saviour

Colin Owen

3 verses

© Copyright 1993 Kingsway's Thankyou Music, P.O. Box 75, Eastbourne,
East Sussex, BN23 6NW, UK. Used by permission.

414 O the deep, deep love of Jesus

Thomas Williams

Music © Copyright control (revived 1996)

415 O the glory of your presence

Steven Fry

416 O thou who camest from above (Tune 1)

Samuel Sebastian Wesley

4 verses

416a O thou who camest from above (Tune 2)

Greenwood's Psalmody, Halifax

4 verses

417 Our confidence is in the Lord

Noel and Tricia Richards

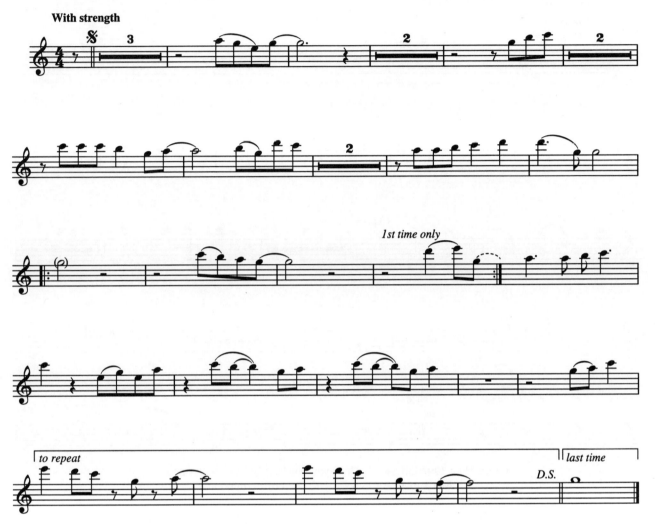

418 Our God is an awesome God
(Awesome God)

Rich Mullins

419 Our God is awesome in power
(Warrior)

Noel and Tricia Richards

2 verses

420 Our God is so great

Unknown

421 Over the mountains and the sea
(I could sing of your love for ever)

Martin Smith

422 Overwhelmed by love

Noel Richards

2 verses

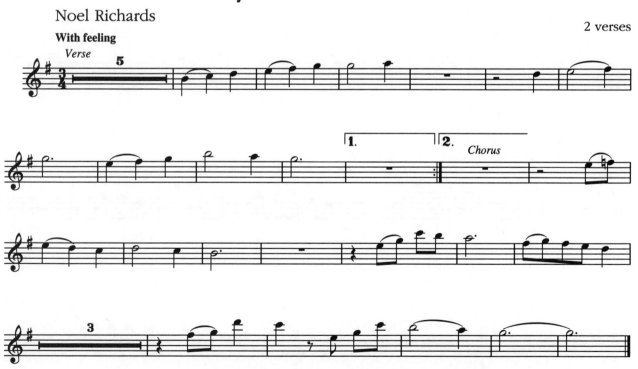

423 O, we are more than conquerors

Steven Fry

424 O, what a morning
(Christ is risen)

Graham Kendrick

2 verses

425 O worship the King

6 verses

William Croft

426 O worship the Lord in the beauty of holiness

Melody from the *Rheinhardt MS,* Üttingen

5 verses

427 Peace be to these streets

Graham Kendrick

4 verses

428 Peace I give to you

Graham Kendrick

6 verses

429 Peace like a river

John Watson

430 Peace, perfect peace

Kevin Mayhew

5 verses

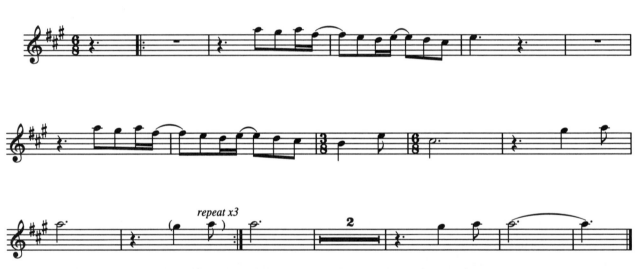

431 Peace to you

Graham Kendrick

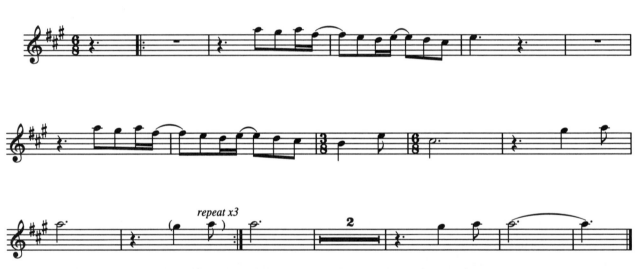

repeat x3

432 Praise God from whom all blessings flow

Andy Piercy and Dave Clifton

Steady rock feel
(play on repeat)   *(both times)*

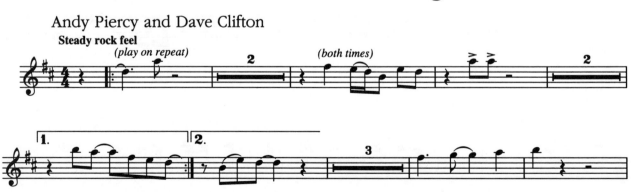

433 Praise, my soul, the King of heaven

John Goss

4 verses

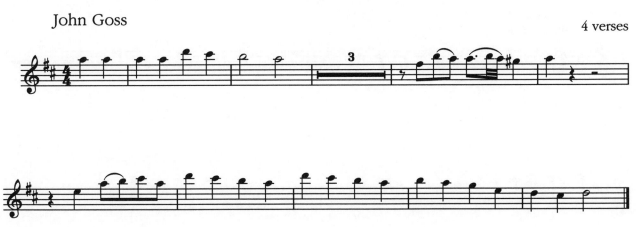

434 Praise the Lord, O my soul

Jeannie Hall and Carol Owen

4 verses

435 Praise the name of Jesus

Roy Hicks

Worshipfully

436 Purify my heart
(Refiner's fire)

Brian Doerksen

2 verses

437 Reign in me

Chris Bowater

438 Rejoice!

Graham Kendrick

3 verses

Triumphantly

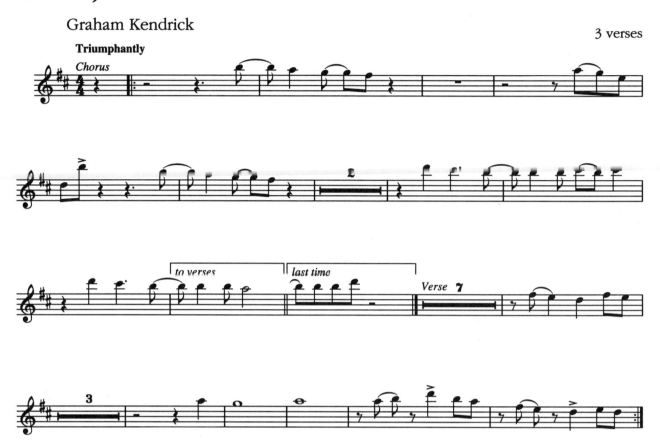

439 Restore, O Lord

Graham Kendrick

4 verses

Steadily, with feeling

440 Righteousness, peace, joy in the Holy Ghost

Helena Barrington

4 verses

With an 'island' feel

441 River, wash over me

Dougie Brown

3 verses

Unhurried, with strength

442 Ruach

David Fellingham

With a sense of awe

443 Salvation belongs to our God

Adrian Howard and Pat Turner

2 verses

444 Save the people

4 verses

Graham Kendrick

445 Say the word

Stuart Townend

3 verses

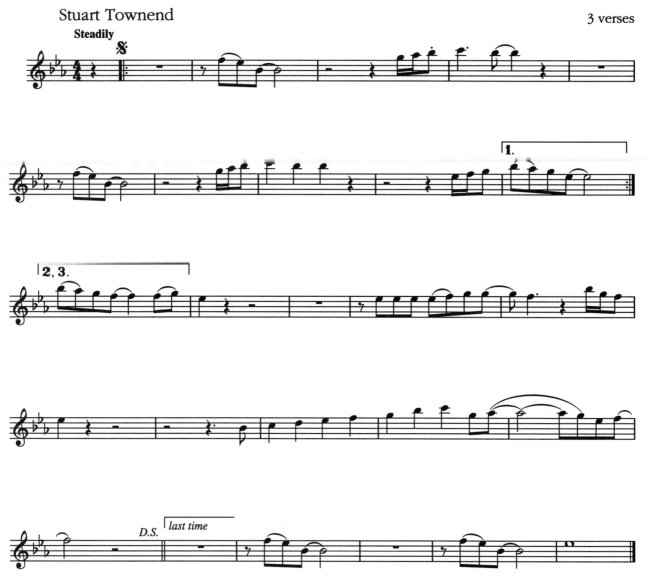

446 See his glory

Chris Bowater

447 Seek ye first

Karen Lafferty

6 verses

Brightly

448 See, your saviour comes

4 verses

Graham Kendrick

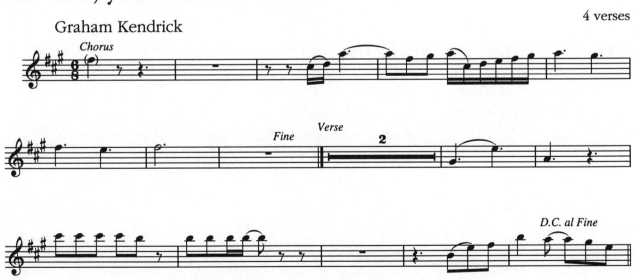

449 Shout for joy

Dave Bilbrough

3 verses

450 Shout for joy and sing

David Fellingham

451 Shout, shout for joy

Dave Bell

452 Shout! The Lord is risen
(The day of his power)
Graham Kendrick

9 verses

453 Shout unto God

Collette Dallas and Deborah Page

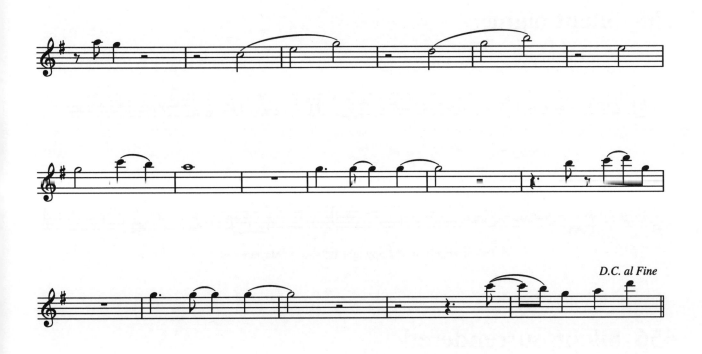

454 Show your power, O Lord

Graham Kendrick

2 verses

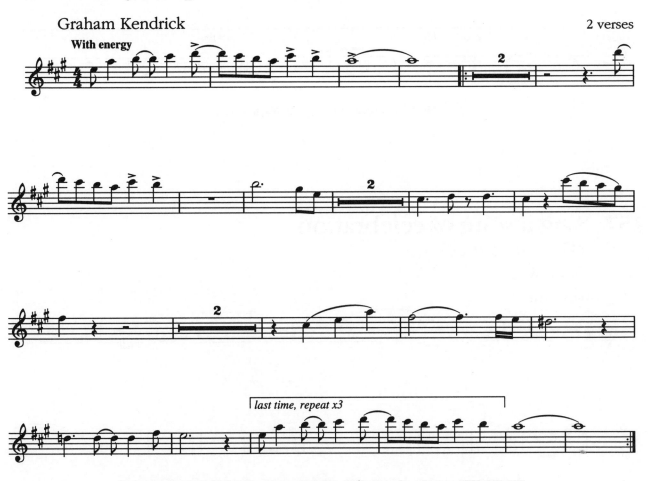

455 Silent night

Franz Grüber

3 verses

456 Silent, surrendered

Margaret Rizza

457 Sing a song of celebration
(We will dance)

David Ruis

458 Sing, praise and bless the Lord
(Laudate Dominum)

Jacques Berthier

459 Soften my heart, Lord

Graham Kendrick

Prayerfully

460 Soon and very soon

Andraé Crouch

3 verses

Rhythmically

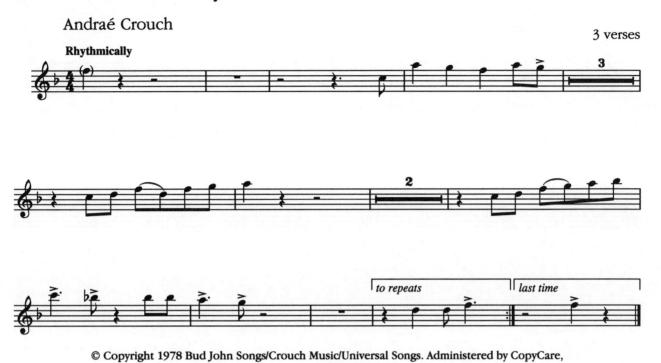

to repeats

last time

461 Sound the trumpet

Dave Bilbrough

Strong and rhythmic

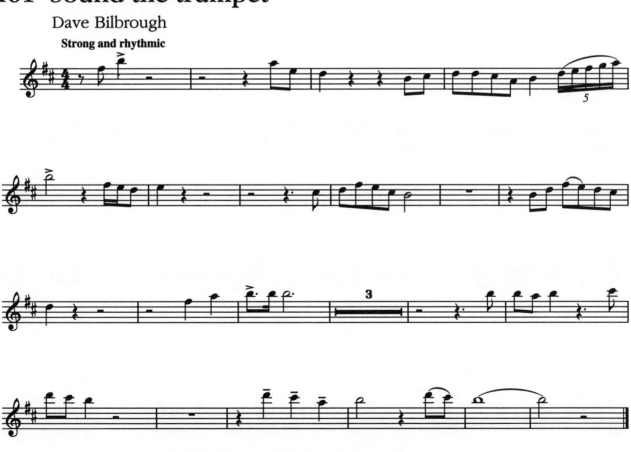

462 Spirit of the living God (Iverson)

Daniel Iverson

463 Spirit of the living God (Armstrong)

Paul Armstrong

464 Streams of worship

David Hadden

3 verses

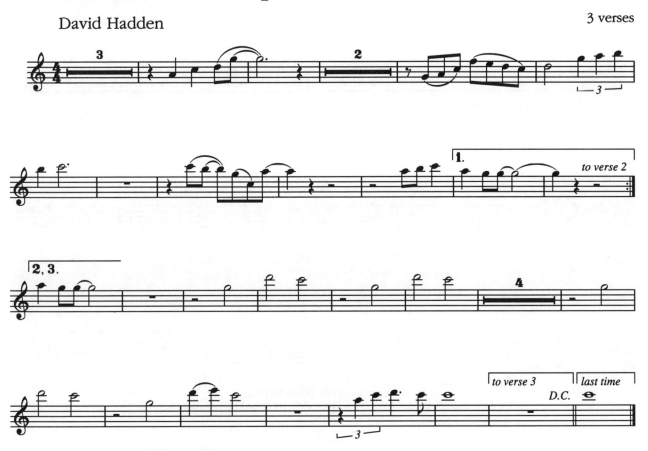

465 Such love

Graham Kendrick

3 verses

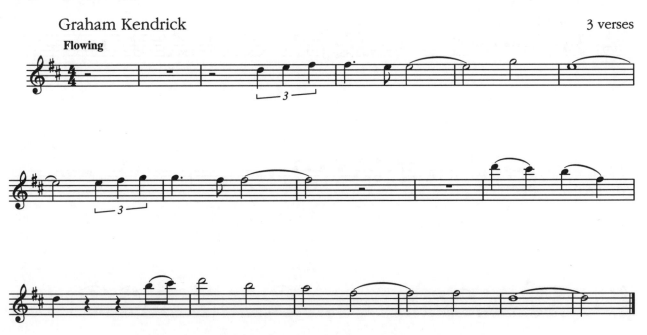

466 Surely our God
(Revealer of mysteries)
David and Liz Morris

3 verses

Chorus

467 Take me past the outer courts
(Take me in)
Dave Browning

Reverently

468 Take my life, and let it be

From *The Parish Choir*

6 verses

468a Take my life, and let it be

Henri A. Cesar Malan

5 verses

469 Teach me to dance

Graham Kendrick

2 verses

470 Teach me your ways
(Purify my heart)

Eugene Greco

471 Tell out, my soul

Walter Greatorex

4 verses

472 Thank you for saving me

Martin Smith

2 verses

With a steady rhythm

473 Thank you for the cross
(O I love you, Lord)

Graham Kendrick

2 verses

Quietly

Brightly

474 Thank you for your mercy
(Great is your mercy)

Don Moen

475 Thank you, Jesus

Unknown

3 verses

476 The angels, Lord, they sing

Matt Redman

3 verses

With awe

477 The church's one foundation

Samuel Sebastian Wesley

4 verses

478 The cross has said it all

Matt Redman and Martin Smith

2 verses

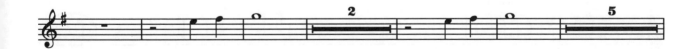

479 The crucible for silver

Martin Smith

With anticipation

480 The heavens shall declare

Geoff Bullock

481 The Lord is a mighty king
(Creation creed)

Graham kendrick

2 verses

482 The Lord is marching out
(O give thanks)

Graham Kendrick

2 verses

March

483 The Lord is moving across this land
(We're in God's army)

Colin Owen

3 verses

484 The Lord is our strength

Colin Owen

2 verses

485 The Lord reigns

Dan C. Stradwick

2 verses

486 The Lord's my shepherd

Jessie Seymour Irvine

5 verses

487 The price is paid

Graham Kendrick

Triumphantly

4 verses

Verse

Chorus   3

to verses

last time

488 The promise of the Holy Spirit
(Acts chapter 2, verse 39)

Richard Hubbard

489 Therefore we lift our hearts in praise
(Version 1)

Unknown

489a Therefore we lift our hearts in praise
(Version 2)
Unknown

6 verses

490 There is a louder shout to come

Matt Redman

3 verses

With conviction

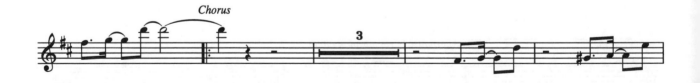

491 There is a place of commanded blessing
(Break dividing walls)
David Ruis

492 There is a Redeemer

Melody Green

3 verses

Hymn-like

493 There is none like you

Lenny LeBlanc

Tenderly

D.C. al Fine

494 There is only one Lord

Morris Chapman and Claire Cloninger

Strong 2-beat gospel feel

Chorus

last time

495 There is power in the name of Jesus

Noel Richards

2 verses

Rocky

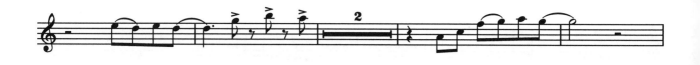

to verse 2 | *last time*

496 There's a blessed time that's coming
(We shall see the King)

J.B. Vaughn

3 verses

497 There's an awesome sound
(Send revival)

Richard Lewis

2 verses

Building in strength

498 There's a place where the streets shine
(Because of you)

Paul Oakley

3 verses

499 There's a river of joy

Taran Ash, James Mott and Matthew Pryce

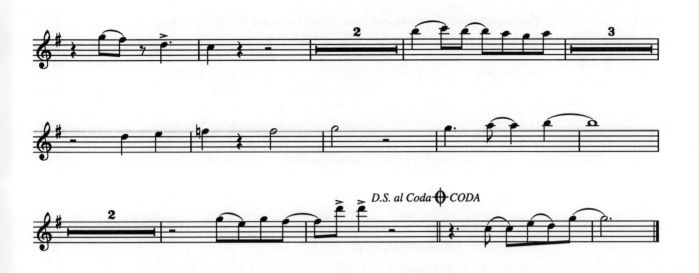

500 There's a sound of singing

Matt Redman and Paul Donnelly

the source will be developed into a major resource for the churches. It is already available in the following editions

Words Only	ISBN	1 84003 121 2
	Catalogue No.	1470101
Full Music	ISBN	1 84003 120 4
	ISMN	M 57004 204 3
	Catalogue No.	1470104
Complete Acetate Masters	ISBN	1 84003 119 0
	Catalogue No.	1470201

Arrangements for Worship Groups:

Book 1 for C instruments	ISBN	1 84003 122 0
	ISMN	M 57004 205 0
	Catalogue No.	1470301
Book 1 for B♭ instruments	ISBN	1 84003 128 X
	ISMN	M 57004 211 1
	Catalogue No.	1470307
Book 2 for C instruments	ISBN	1 84003 123 9
	ISMN	M 57004 206 7
	Catalogue No.	1470302
Book 2 for B♭ instruments	ISBN	1 84003 129 8
	ISMN	M 57004 212 8
	Catalogue No.	1470308
Book 3 for C instruments	ISBN	1 84003 124 7
	ISMN	M 57004 207 4
	Catalogue No.	1470303
Book 3 for B♭ instruments	ISBN	1 84003 130 1
	ISMN	M 57004 213 5
	Catalogue No.	1470309
Book 4 for C instruments	ISBN	1 84003 125 5
	ISMN	M 57004 208 1
	Catalogue No.	1470304
Book 4 for B♭ instruments	ISBN	1 84003 131 X
	ISMN	M 57004 214 2
	Catalogue No.	1470310
Book 5 for C instruments	ISBN	1 84003 126 3
	ISMN	M 57004 209 8
	Catalogue No.	1470305
Book 5 for B♭ instruments	ISBN	1 84003 132 8
	ISMN	M 57004 215 9
	Catalogue No.	1470311